Blended, But Not Broken

Blended, But Not Broken

Billy Dee & Tanisha Williams

XULON PRESS

Xulon Press
2301 Lucien Way #415
Maitland, FL 32751
407.339.4217
www.xulonpress.com

© 2019 by Billy Dee Williams & Tanisha Williams

All rights reserved solely by the author. The author guarantees all contents are original and do not infringe upon the legal rights of any other person or work. No part of this book may be reproduced in any form without the permission of the author. The views expressed in this book are not necessarily those of the publisher.

Unless otherwise indicated, Scripture quotations taken from the King James Version (KJV) – public domain.

Printed in the United States of America.

ISBN-13: 978-1-5456-7879-4

Table of Contents

Dedication vii
Acknowledgments ix
Author's Note to the Readers xi
Preface xiii
Introduction xv

1. Things You Should Know Before Committing to a
   Blended Family 1
2. No Step Here! 7
3. Investment 13
4. Love Has Everything to Do with Blended Families 19
5. Because the Family Structure Looks Different, the
   Principle Should Look How God Intended 29
6. The Challenges With Blended Families 37
7. One-on-One Time With Your Bio-Child 41
8. Let the Bio Do the Discipline 47
9. Never Compete With the Other Parent 51
10. Family Meeting Bridge the Gaps 55
11. The Importance of Family Vacations 59
12. You Can Be Blended and Not Broken 63
13. From the Children's Perspective 65

Dedication

This book is dedicated to my mother, Phyllis Loraine Robertson, whose love, discipline, and loving nature has developed me into the man that I am today.

Acknowledgments

To our Love Oasis Ministries Family, we say thank you for your continuous love, support, and prayers. Together, we will continue to nurture people by building families and love them back to life.

We want to thank our sister, LaTaveya Vault, for all the time spent in editing our final draft of the book. We appreciate you!

We want to thank Jason Long, President of J.L. Designs Creative Group in Chicago, IL, for the creation of our remarkable book over. We appreciate your gift! We want to thank our sister-friend, Kathy Rodriquez, for her continual seeds sown, prayers, and support.

We want to thank our spiritual parents, Pastor Alvin & Rochelle Robertson, for believing in us and encouraging us to go forward with the blended family teachings.

A special thank you to our children for being patient with us and loving us through our flaws. We love you all; your love and support mean everything to us.

Above all, we thank our Heavenly Father, who has made all of this possible.

Thank you, Lord, for using us for your glory.

Author's Note to the Readers

We are writing this book to prayerfully help families that may be living in a blended family situation and don't have a clue on what to do or how to handle family dynamics or emotional issues. In the beginning, we didn't know what to do or what to say. Nor did we have a resource to turn to for good godly advice concerning blended families. In our eyes, we didn't see anyone doing it right.

This book is not the Bible, but we have used many biblical principles. Applying these principles has completely changed our lives. Our whole focus of this book is to help others make their marriages and families better.

In our most challenging times, the Lord spoke in many ways and declared that our family would be an example to many others. It has not been easy, but it's been worth it every step of the way. I've learned so much, and I wouldn't be the man I am today if I hadn't experienced a blended family. Our belief is, if one family can benefit from our adventures, then the process of writing and publishing this book will be worth it.

Enjoy the behind-the-scenes life of the Williams family.

Billy's two girls: Tyana and Kyara.

Tanisha's two girls and boy: Shakerra, Byrianna, and Byron Jr.

Preface

April 6, 2003, was the day Billy and I exchanged phone numbers. The thought ran through our mind, "who's gonna call who first?" The next day I'm at home wondering, "is Billy going to call, should I call him, or let him chase?" Mind you, Billy's at work just as scared, wondering whether he should call or wait until I call. Finally, I said to myself, "Self, you don't have time to be playing games, just call the man." So I did. I made the first move, and Billy was relieved.

April 8, 2003, Billy drove thirty minutes to see me for about fifteen minutes before his forty-minute drive to work. We would talk or see each other every day from that day on. Either he would drive thirty minutes to see me before work, or I would drive thirty minutes to be with him before work, and many times, I wouldn't make it into work. We were falling in love and weren't even thinking about what the kids were thinking or feeling. After four months into the relationship, we knew we wanted to spend the rest of our lives together.

The Proposal: December 2003 marked eight months of being together. Billy and I were ready to go to the next stage in our relationship. One day, I approached Billy's Aunt Allison and told her that I wanted to propose to Billy. I proposed the idea of having a Christmas party at her house with some friends and family. I had planned to purchase the decorations and food to make it beautiful. I also told her I wanted to fly Billy's mom in and surprise him with her at the same time. Aunt Allison was excited and willing to help me pull everything off. Little did I know, Billy went to the same aunt and told her he wanted to propose to me. He had the same idea of a Christmas party at her house, even the part where he desired to fly my dad in from Florida so he could be here for the occasion. We both told his sister, Tay, what we were planning, and she wanted to be here too. No one spoiled the surprise! I was able to fly his mom in from Arkansas, but my dad couldn't get off work, so Billy couldn't fly him in. However, Billy drove to Arkansas to pick his sister up so she wouldn't miss the big day.

The night arrived, the time had come, and I was so nervous. Allison quieted the room, got everyone's attention, and then, Billy stood up. My face was confused. I didn't know what was going on. Billy got on his knee, said how much he loved me, what he thought about me as a woman and a mother. Next, he asked me to marry him. I was crying as he put the ring on my finger; I didn't even look at the ring. I was trying to get myself together because it was my turn now. The family was clapping and cheering, and then it calmed down again. Shocked, nervous, and with tears running down my face, I got my words out and asked Billy to marry me. Of course, he said, "YES."

That was how it all began.

Introduction

Tanisha:

A blended family...what is that? I had never heard of it until my *blend* began. I didn't have a clue what to do. I'd heard about stepmothers, stepfathers, and stepsisters, of course. I was programmed to think if you weren't from the line of Louis Hayes Jr., you were not part of my family.

When I was eleven, the trouble started—my parents divorced. I am a daddy's girl to my heart. *My daddy was stripped away from me by this lady who he had the nerve to marry.* Those were my thoughts as an eleven-year-old girl. My life was changed forever from this one act of selfishness.

I'd never seen my parents argue. All I remember is love being in my home. Then one day, I came home, and it was all over. This other lady was pregnant by my father, who was still married to my mom.

My feelings, it seemed, were not relevant to anyone. I became bitter, angry, confused, frustrated, and disconnected. I never called my dad's wife, my mom or stepmom; I would say, Mrs. (Blank). Her kids were her kids, but the two my daddy had with her were my brothers. I love my brothers, don't get me wrong. I never was disrespectful, and I had nothing against her kids—we just never blended.

I would use my dad's wife to get what I wanted. Since I was my dad's only daughter and a daddy's girl, the woman tried to get close to me. My dad has never put any of his wives before me.

My dad married two more times after that first lady, and they both had even more kids. I didn't like any of the wives, especially wife number three. Her kids put my dad through hell, and I couldn't stand them. I just wanted to be with my dad, so I dealt with all their dirty, nasty, and disrespectful situations.

As I grew older, my family situation began to change. I had my first child at the tender age of fifteen. A teenage girl, just broken and looking for love in all the wrong places—that was me. When my daughter, Kerra, was three years old, I started dating my ex-husband. He was excellent with her; he loved her as his own. However, his mother wasn't fond of her son being with a ready-made family, and that led to resentment.

I was only twenty-one years old, and my ex-husband was twenty when we got married. We were both clueless—had no idea what we were doing. The blend for Kerra and us was fine, but it was war with his mom. She refused to accept three-year-old Kerra. This situation was new for us all. We did the best we could with what we knew.

Introduction

Billy:

When I was born, my family was already participating in a blended family relationship. Growing up, my dad had been part of a blended family. He has two older half-brothers—the same mother, but they had a different father. My mother's dad was the oldest of his blended family. His dad (my great-grandfather) had two other families that I know of, but my grandfather and his half-brother have the same first name—by two different mothers.

When I was younger, Dad's brothers and sisters would come down from Chicago, or he would go up there to visit. I never understood the situation until I was much older. The man who'd raised Dad, his stepfather, treated him like his own son. Dad had great respect, love for him, and I never heard any horror stories concerning their relationship.

Now, as far as my childhood, I knew growing up, I had two older sisters, who are twins, on my father's side. When I was six, my mom had a second child by another man. She seemed like my first "real" sibling, since we lived in the same house, even though we had different fathers.

By the time I was sixteen, I had three more siblings. My mother had, altogether, four baby daddies. I got along with everyone, even my father. They all played a significant role in my life and helped form my personality—helped me become the man I am today.

My dad got married and had another child with his wife. She already had two kids when he married her. So, my father had three baby moms, four kids, and two stepchildren he was trying to raise.

My mom ended up marrying my baby sister's father—he already had four kids. From a child's viewpoint, this was the first time I can remember my mother trying to blend her kids with someone else's kids. From my perspective, the kids' relationships were amazingly free of tension and melodrama. I have a stepbrother about a year younger than me; we became best friends and have maintained a close relationship because of our childhood. With my father's stepchildren, they were like blood, sisters, and brothers. Our relationships couldn't have been any better. I still love them from the bottom of my heart.

My twin sisters, on my dad's side, always lived elsewhere. Their mom was in the military, so I hardly ever saw them. Despite the reality that we didn't see much of each other, my love for them was great. What I did know is that there was an eight months difference in age between my twin sisters and myself.

My mom's third baby-dad had children of his own, but he and my mother didn't stay together long enough for us to gel. I didn't know the kids, but I knew of them.

So, many years later, I never thought it would be a problem for me to have a stepchild since I'd come through so many stepsibling situations. The ones I was able to form relationships with were great experiences. I almost encouraged blended families until I went through it myself.

When I met Tanisha, she had three children, and I immediately thought, "Now, that's too many. One child is only three months old. Loose here, Satan, I'm not going to be able to do this." My second thought was similar. "Umm, never mind, I am not equipped for all of this." In fact, her uncle, who later became my pastor, said, "You must look past that." I was like, "I can't see that far—*three kids!*" But she was what I'd prayed for and MORE. "Lord, help me."

I began to think she'd only had two baby-dads, and one hadn't really been in the picture. So I'd only have to deal with one joker. "I can, at least, try it," I thought. I'd just turned twenty-six, and I thought I was ready to settle down and have a family, but, boy, did I have a rude awakening. At this point, I was having the worst baby-momma drama of my life, not being able to see my kids while living in the same town. I didn't know if I was coming or going. Later I realized, I needed Tanisha and the kids to give me hope because, without them, I probably would have lost my mind. (That's about all I had left anyway). The having-my-own-family thing was new in my life, but I thought, "This can be great if I can just endure the unknown."

Until that point in my life, I'd never heard any messages in a church concerning blended families or having stepchildren. I neither knew nor witnessed anyone doing it right, concerning living in a blended family, so the struggle was real.

Nobody but God equipped our kids and us to have the success we've had. We still have issues, but each time, we don't stay there as long as the previous issue.

For this reason, we are writing this book. We wish to use our experiences to help you and many others. God said we would be an example to the body of Christ.

CHAPTER 1

Things You Should Know Before Committing to a Blended Family

Billy:

*T*here are a lot of factors that impact success in a blended family — such as age, culture, individual belief system, and so much more. There are also external factors, such as what society has to say concerning this situation.

Most relationships seem to "just *happen*." However, most people don't take into account the statistics of a blended family. We join into a blended family because we like the other woman or man and find them attractive. Eventually, the two adults fall in love. Prayerfully, it works out. Most people in relationships never really try to examine the upbringing of the other person and how they genuinely feel about blending the two families.

Most couples head into blending their separate families cluelessly, never really understanding how to make them work. I believe prayer must be the foundation in committing to a blended family environment. If you have a whole lot of baggage or issues—and no one likes to admit that stuff in the beginning—it will take a toll on the relationship and, especially, on the blended family.

I suggest spending more intimate time with God while facing your shortcomings as a person. The time spent with God will bring about additional personal development. Another benefit is it will do wonders for strengthening your relationship with your love and your new blended family. What you don't know really can hurt you.

What is a Blended Family?

So what exactly is a blended family? According to the Oxford Dictionary, a blended family is a family consisting of a couple and their children from this and all previous relationships.

Statistics of Blended Families

Stepfamilies are not addressed, assessed, and counted—further catapulting those who live in and lead our society into the quagmire of ignorance. The numbers, however, tell the story:

The **US Bureau of Census** relates:

- 1,300 new stepfamilies are formed every day.
- Over 50% of US families are remarried or re-coupled.
- The average marriage in America lasts only seven years.
- One out of two marriages ends in divorce.
- 75% remarry.
- 66% of those living together—or remarried—break up when children are involved.

- 80% of remarried, or re-coupled, partners with children both have careers.
- 50% of the sixty million children under the age of thirteen are currently living with one biological parent and that parent's current partner.
- The 1990 US Census stated there would be more stepfamilies than original families by the year 2000.
- According to the **Stepfamily Foundation's** research, more than 60% of divorced fathers visit their children. These children do not legally "reside" with their fathers. So, neither government nor academic research includes these fathers and their children as stepfamilies. The father may be a single dad, but most likely, he has re-coupled or remarried, thus creating a stepfamily. These children shuttle between their parent's homes, radically increasing the numbers of stepfamilies. These fathers are ignored and uncounted.
- 75% of stepfamilies complain of "not having access to resources as a stepfamily," according to a recent Stepfamily Foundation survey of 2,000 web questionnaires.
- A Boston University psychologist researcher reported that 75% of career women who earned over $100,000 and had married men with children said that If they do it again, they would NOT marry a man with children."
- 50% of all women, not just mothers, are likely sometime in their lives to live in a stepfamily relationship, especially when we include living-together families in our definition of the stepfamily, according to research compiled by Professor of Sociology, Larry L. Bumpass, of the University of Wisconsin.
- Only 45 percent of children "do well" after divorce.

- 41% of these children are doing poorly, underachieving, worried, deprecating, and often angry.
- 50% of divorced women and 30% of divorced men were still intensely bitter with their former spouses.
- Most felt the lack of a template, a working model, for a loving relationship between a man and a woman.
- Divorced parents provide less time, less discipline, and are less sensitive to the children as they are caught up in their divorce and its aftermath.
- Many parents are unable to separate their needs from the children's needs. They often share too much of their personal life with their children, placing the children in a precarious emotional state. The children are also vulnerable to grandiosity or to depression within what is left of their families.
- Most parents from divorced homes are chronically disorganized and unable to parent effectively.
- As diminished parenting continues, it permanently disrupts the child's once "normal" emotional growth and functioning.
- The good news, according to the study: "The children of divorce tended to do well if mothers and fathers, regardless of remarriage, resumed parenting roles, putting differences aside and allowing the children to continue relationships with both parents.

Other effects on children:

1. Most children are doing reasonably well within two years of the divorce.
2. About 25% of youths from divorced families have serious social or emotional problems; 10% of intact families do.
3. Most young adults from divorce are establishing careers, creating intimate relationships, and building meaningful lives.
4. Young women do better than young men, often becoming more competent than if they had stayed in unhappy family situations; some thrive.
5. 70% of adult children of divorce say divorce is an acceptable solution to an unhappy marriage, even with children; 40% from non-divorced families agree.

CHAPTER 2

No Step Here!

Billy:

What you call your new kids is so important when you blend families with your partner.

> **Genesis 2:19-20**
> *19 "And out of the ground the LORD God formed every beast of the field, and every fowl of the air; and <u>brought them unto Adam to see what he would call them: and whatsoever Adam called every living creature, that was the name thereof.</u> 20 And Adam gave names to all cattle, and to the fowl of the air, and to every beast of the field; but for Adam there was not found a help meet for him."*

In so many relationships, I see and hear many people say those are *his* kids, or those are *her* kids and never take ownership. Ultimately, they treat each other's kids differently than their biological children.

Many don't understand the magnitude of naming your kids or what you call them. Anytime you name something, you have established dominion and are responsible for them. That's why God brought the animals unto Adam to see what he would call them.

I mentioned earlier I'd been raised in a blended family. I'd never heard my father call his brothers, *stepbrothers*. Concerning my grandpa, with the many siblings he'd had growing up as stepbrothers or sisters, I knew no difference between the blood relationships and the stepfamily members. When I found out, they'd already been my uncle or aunt for years. Regardless, what is a step-uncle or step-aunt? It sounds crazy.

When the time came that I mentally and spiritually knew Tanisha would be my wife, it wasn't long afterward we talked on the phone. I knew what I called her kids would be so important.

To be perfectly honest, I called them *my kids* from day one. The only time I said stepchildren was to explain to people how I had so many kids of my age, which I appeared to be. When I tell others how old I am and how old Shakerra is, to this day, they immediately try to figure out how old I was when she was born. Then, I have to explain to people that when I met my wife, she had three children, and I had two children, and that's how we ended up with five.

I never use the word *step*. I didn't know why it was this way for me—I just didn't do it. Later, I found out it was the Holy Spirit leading me and guiding me.

No Step Here!

The word stepchild has come off as a bad word. I would hear people say, "Beat you like a stepchild." Or "You look like a red-headed stepchild," which derives from an old tale of a woman who'd stepped out of her relationship, then had a child who looked like the out-of-wedlock father. Over the years, and even until this day, people don't claim their spouse's children, and, if they do, it's their step-child.

According to Websters New World College Dictionary, the word STEP-comes from the old English word Steop and Steop means *"something that does not receive appropriate care, respect, or attention."* Merriam-Webster Dictionary states the word *step-child* means *"related by marriage rather than blood."*

I didn't know this at the time, but I didn't like that word. These are my kids, and that settles it. I love them no differently than my children who share my DNA. I don't know, but the way my heart is set up, I believe, I'm just a little different. Blame it on God.

When I met Tyana, my oldest of the two, she was in her mother's womb. I decided right then that I would give her appropriate care, respect, and attention. We have no blood relation, but, in this case, love is thicker than blood. I took ownership of her in her mother's womb, and I loved her from the start. I still do as if I'd helped create her. It was later in life when I begin to tell people that we shared no DNA, just G-O-D, it was because I didn't want anyone to treat her differently. I learned then if I can love that child, surely, I can love someone else's the same way.

But many people grow up in a stepfamily environment, and it doesn't go well because of what the word *step* means, which is something that does not receive appropriate care, respect, or attention. This is why I believe in order for the family to grow, what you call, the children is critically important.

Now, when I hear the word *step*, I cringe because I know people don't know what it means though they continue to say it. The truth of the matter is, when you use the word *step*, you can't love that person the way you should because you have downgraded them. They won't get the appropriate care, respect, or attention because you have created a mental block, and you don't even know it.

What the children call me is not nearly as important as what I call them. At the current time, my two oldest kids, Shakerra and Byrianna, still don't call me dad or father. Now, Byron, because I have been in his life since he was three months old, he calls me dad. What's funny, I've never told him to call me dad. In fact, when he would go to his birth father's house, he would get in trouble for calling me, dad. What his birth-father didn't understand was that I gave my son or his son, now our son, the appropriate care, respect, and attention when he wasn't there—so I've earned the right to be called dad in the child's eyes. In time, the child will have resentment toward his birth father because he was making him choose, and the child didn't ask to be put into that situation.

My oldest two children call me Mr. Billy because that's what they were taught, and it was totally out of respect. Now, because we know each other a little more, I have graduated to Co-Parent.

Before, it was like this, "My mom and my stepdad." Now it's just, "My parents said this or that."

Your job as the incoming partner is to treat your partner's children no differently than your own. It will be challenging if your biological kids are giving you the appropriate care, respect, attention, and the others are not. But keep reading—the next chapter will bless you.

Famous quote
"The only steps in the house are the stair steps, and the only half in this house is half-and-half creamer." (Al Hodson)

CHAPTER 3

Investment

Billy:

I believe this works with any child who is under the age of eighteen.

Always Remember This:
It's an investment that you might not see a return on right away.

Investment-*"investment is the purchase of goods that are not consumed today but are used in the future to create wealth."* *(Chen, J., Investopia, 2019)*

> **Genesis 8:22 KJV**
> **22** *"While the earth remaineth, seedtime and harvest, and cold and heat, and summer and winter, and day and night shall not cease."*

Me, having grown up with many men in my life and even a stepmother, I never thought that having a stepchild or stepchildren would be difficult. I knew, going into the relationship that I had to love her children as my own. So, I was committed to that from the beginning. I spent quality time with each of them, individually, because I wanted them to understand I genuinely loved them.

My other goal was to help them understand that having another man in their life can be difficult. While I wasn't trying to replace their Dad, I wanted them to know it was important for me to help each child in any aspect that I could.

It's imperative to come in as a role model or a friend, investing a lot of time and energy. You need to figure out what each child likes and support them to the fullest, even if you know nothing about their hobbies, even if you're not interested in what they are doing. Again, it's called an *investment*. The more time you invest, the smoother this process will work.

It's my firm belief that *seedtime followed by harvest time; the relationship grows at its best when you water it properly.*

Shakerra, being the oldest (I believe she was twelve-years-old)—at that time was playing softball. I would drive thirty to forty minutes to most games or practices to invest in what she liked or was doing. Well, my being a sports fanatic made that easy. I was already coaching little league football in another city, but my love for sports was at an all-time high. By the way, it still is.

Well, what I knew from the Holy Spirit was that my *investment* would be critical in building a relationship with these children. In fact, it became the catalyst for our relationships because they loved sports too. I had the pleasure of being all my children's coaches and, for some, their first coach. To this day, all my children are live-hard Dallas Cowboys fans because of the investment I'd made when they were younger. (Oh, yeah, I had to throw that in there.) All of them are sports fans of some sort, and it's mostly the girls.

The investments are not easy—it is a very sacrificial effort. As the children began to grow older, the time I put in was not appreciated. I thought they should have said thank you more often. We had conversations concerning that because I felt what I'd done was in vain. There were times I had to go to five games in one day because all my kids were playing sports in different places at the same time. When they'd see me (my stepchildren), they had a stank face when looking at me. I found out later that they wanted their father there and they already knew I'd be there. At that point, it wasn't even about me, but I took it personally and got upset because I didn't understand the investment and I wanted my praise *now* and *not later,* In the spiritual sense, you see, I tried to plant the seed and receive my harvest the same day I'd planted it.

In the investment process, you can't have ulterior motives because, in due time, you will be mentally and physically drained. That will cause a hardship on the new relationship or marriage.

Notice in this whole chapter that I am talking about investment—I never brought up my wife, Tanisha's name. That's because the investment has nothing to do with the spouse or the counterpart. In fact, the other person must get out of the way when the new parent is building a relationship.

I see too many people get in the way or become overprotective of their children, and never allow the other person to build or *invest* in the new family. To be truthful, that stunts the growth of the family. If you don't trust them, why are they there anyway? I'm just saying.

Both parties must understand the process and know that it takes time. *Do not* uproot the seed before you water it.

What typically happens is, in most relationships, the partners don't invest time in each other before introducing the other adult to the kids. The other person is being watched continually because, at this point in the relationship, you don't trust that person to be alone with your kids. So again, why are they there? Before you can invest time in the children, you *must* invest time in each other. I've said the same thing two or three times in the same sentence because we don't get it. We've become thirsty in search of a relationship, that we bring anybody around our kids too early. Then we expect it to work like a well-oiled machine.

In the investment stage, you need to ask does he or she have kids? How is the relationship between them? These questions are essential because you can *have* kids and not *raise* them. Then, they are practicing on yours. NO!

How you discipline your children needs to be talked about in the investment stage with each other *before you meet each other's kids*. I know this may seem redundant, but many will read this while they are in a full-blown relationship, pulling their hair out, wondering why their marriage and partnerships are not working. It's because they have never invested time in each other and discussed discipline *first*.

Investment

In marriage counseling sessions, we have done with blended families; most of the spouses struggle in investing in each other. If you add anything else to this equation, it's going to be chaotic. I said all that to say this: if there is *no real investment* in love, it's going to be challenging to invest in anything else.

Chapter 4

Love Has Everything to Do with Blended Families

Billy:

Love Must be the Foundation!

> **Mark 12:29-31**
> *29 "And Jesus answered him, The first of all the commandments is, Hear, O Israel; The Lord our God is one Lord: 30 And thou shalt love the Lord thy God with all thy heart, and with all thy soul, and with all thy mind, and with all thy strength: this is the first commandment. 31 And the second is like, namely this, Thou shalt love thy neighbor as thyself. There is none other commandment greater than these."*

I had the honor of working with my grandfather growing up. His occupation was a contractor with the expertise of finishing concrete. I think he worked on over 1,000 homes, colleges, supermarkets, fast food restaurants you name it. Anything that needed a strong foundation, we did it. My grandfather laid foundations for over forty years, and we, as a family, still do it until this present day. Not one foundation we did has depleted. In fact, some structures have burned to the foundation remained. If the foundation is right, you can build on it. So, love must be the foundation, and many blended families are not built on the true agape love foundation.

People know when you don't like them and if you don't love them, especially children. In most cases, children are the innocent ones. I said *most cases*, or should I say *some cases*. Well, love is an *action* word, and it is the greatest commandment. A lot of times, I see adults take their anger and frustration out on the kids and, the truth of the matter is, the kids never asked to be in the situation in the first place. In some cases, all they want is their biological mom and dad together and don't understand why they are not. So naturally, if there is no communication, they are automatically going to think the new spouse is the reason their parents are not together, and in some cases, that is true.

When growing up, I went through a phase in my life where all I wanted was my dad. I didn't care who my mother was with. I'd think to myself, "If my mom weren't with this guy, maybe my dad would have a chance to come back." I would cry so much because I missed my dad, and I longed to have both parents at home with me. I couldn't figure out why they weren't together, and I began to feel resentment toward my mother and any man she brought around me.

I would think, "She doesn't want me happy. What about me and how I feel?" At that time, I only saw my dad on weekends—his choosing; she never kept me away from him. Now, remember, I was going through a phase.

I believe my mom and dad broke up when I was two. During my phase, I was about nine with two other siblings. My mom was with *their* dad and was hardly thinking about *my dad*. What's funny is my dad was married to another woman. Looking back, I think to myself, "Silly Billy" because I had no clue. My point is, one never gives much thought to how the children are and what they're going through. That's why it is *your job* to be Christ-like and to love. It's imperative to have a relationship with God so you can love like Christ. The love of Christ must be in you, and only then can you draw on Christ so you can invest in others.

Again, my grandfather loved his siblings so much that I knew nothing regarding who were blood relatives and who wasn't. That's what love does. It doesn't separate, and it draws people closer together.

> **Jeremiah 31:3**
> *3 "The LORD hath appeared of old unto me, saying, Yea, I have loved thee with an everlasting love: therefore, with lovingkindness have I drawn thee."*

When I met my new blended family, I gave them the last I had to offer. I hardly ever told them *no* and, if I promised them anything, I would do my best to fulfill my promise because, ultimately, I am the example on the earth concerning God. There are so many things we deserve and don't deserve but, because of God's love towards us, He makes it happen. His grace is enough. You don't have to like the children but, if you are consistent in your love, you can't help but like them. Someone has to be the mature one and ten out ten times; it will not be the kids. That means you need to grow up and understand these kids have a mother or father or other relatives who could be feeding them negative information. Still, your job is to love.

> **1 Peter 4:8**
> *8 "And above all things have fervent charity among yourselves: for charity shall cover the multitude of sins."*

It doesn't matter what the children are growing through; love can cover all. You must be sensitive enough to understand that everybody is going through changes, and it's not fair to make them pick or choose or to bottle up their emotions. The truth of the matter is, the children are still trying to figure out what happened. Why Mommy doesn't love Daddy and why Daddy doesn't like Mommy? The children are merely confused. What's crazier is, most people don't know the root cause of why they don't like each other.

Love has everything to do with a blended family.

> **Ephesians 4:2**
> *With all lowliness and meekness, with long-suffering, forbearing one another in love.*

Too many times, people want to fix the kids. The kids are not the problem. It's the parents who have the pain and brokenness. Your pain and your brokenness have been transferred down to your kids, which is called a generational curse. The major problem we are having is too many people are getting this information after they've decided to be with each other.

> **1 Corinthians 13:4-8**
> *4 "Charity suffereth long, and is kind; charity envieth not; charity vaunteth not itself, is not puffed up, 5 Doth not behave itself unseemly, seeketh not her own, is not easily provoked, thinketh no evil; 6 Rejoiceth not in iniquity, but rejoiceth in the truth; 7 Beareth all things, believeth all things, hopeth all things, endureth all things.*
> *8 Charity never faileth: but whether there be prophecies, they shall fail; whether there be tongues, they shall cease; whether there be knowledge, it shall vanish away."*

When we understand the true essence of love, everything takes its proper course depending on the maturity of the individual. Love is, ultimately, a choice. You must choose to love period. Love is not based on what you can get out of it. In fact, the children may never like you, for whatever reason, but you still must choose to love. It's not always going to feel good, but you can't let your feelings get in the way or dictate what is going on during the moment. Sometimes, you might have to take the back seat for a while until they come back around, but until then, your love can't change—you must stay pure and represent Christ at all times.

I know you are going to feel like you are a fool, and think, "I'm not putting up with this." One of the biggest lies we tell ourselves is, "I don't care." But if you didn't care, you wouldn't feel this way.

Shakerra, "my ace boon coon," (the oldest child who I'd invested so much time and energy in) and I had broken up, mainly because of my immaturity. I wasn't able to adapt to her growing up and having her own feelings too. She was graduating from beauty school, and I was so bitter that I robbed her and myself from experiencing her accomplishment. I haven't really told anyone, until now, that I was heartbroken that I'd acted in such an unloving way. My actions weren't pleasing to God or myself. It was so selfish of me to be so worried about how I felt that I couldn't exemplify His love (1 Cor. 13:4-8).

Later, she went to a missionary school in North Carolina. Even though our relationship wasn't like it had been, God gave me another chance and used me to show His love. This time, I didn't let Him down. I drove her and her friend to school, all the way to North Carolina. I put aside my personal feelings and allowed God to be glorified. More importantly, she knew I loved her because love is shown through action. Wait—it gets better. After she completed missionary school, she moved back home. We apologized, and our relationship was rekindled, just like before, until she married. To God, be the glory.

Tanisha:

Love being the foundation was going to be easy for me, or so I figured. My initial thoughts: "First of all, I love kids. Billy has two beautiful little girls with pretty hair." I was so excited. Then, I was like, "We're not going to have any baby momma drama because he's been apart from her for over two years. Oh yes, this is going to be easy." Ha, ha, ha… Little did I know.

Here's one thing about me, I am a disciplinarian. I love kids, but I don't play with them, either. I can't do grown behind kids (kids who think they are grown). I'm old school, so I believe a child should stay in a child's place. My kids weren't my friends; I am their mother. My assignment is to "train them up in the way that they should go, in the fear of God" (Prov. 22:6).

I've said all that to say: I had a challenge on my hands with my new baby girls. When Billy and I first met, his children were the tender ages of three and five. They were just as cute as they could be. What I always had to remind myself was that they are children.

Our baby girl, Kyara, was the one who expanded my prayer life. She was a feisty, smart-mouthed little three-year-old. Thank God I love kids and understand the dynamics. Yet, it was still challenging at times. I understood she was just a child repeating what she had heard—*with an attitude,* mind you. She would say things like, "My momma said you ain't our mom." I'd take a deep breath before responding to her. Then I'd answer, "She's absolutely right, but I'm going to help your Dad in any way he needs me to with you girls."

Remember, I told you I can't stand grown behind kids. I had to keep reminding myself that she was only repeating what she was exposed to. I understood and kept praying it would get better after a while.

I'm not sure if we mentioned this, but Billy and I were living together before we got married. Sooo, I was playing wife *before* I was a wife. (*Sidebar Ladies:* Not a good look. Don't play yourself.)

Okay, back to the story. Growing up, I was the only girl among six brothers. I'd always wanted a sister, but that never happened. However, I thought I was grown would go out and had my daughter at the tender young age of fifteen. Then, five years later, I had another daughter. I share all that to say this: I was not new at knowing how to take care of little girls. As a matter of fact, I was excited about my four little girls.

I loved doing their hair, especially Tyana's and Kyara's; they had some long, pretty hair. One day, as I was doing Tyana's hair, Kyara said, "My momma said don't put that gel in our hair. My momma said You put the rubber bands in our hair too tight.'" It was, "My momma said… my momma said… my momma said…" This continued until, one day, I said to Billy, "I'm not doing their hair anymore. However they come over; that's just how they are going to look, for church and everything." I meant that! The way their hair is set up, it needs to get done every two days, at least. They have that pretty, soft, spider web-type hair.

They would come over, and it looked as if they had been wearing that one hairstyle all week. Their ponytails would have cotton all around the band. I would feel bad taking them places with their hair looking all crazy, but I was acting immature at that moment. I never would take my girls anywhere, looking crazy while I'm all fly. My kids represent me. I had gotten very frustrated with the situation, and I took it out on the kids. I did it a few times until one day, Billy said, "Baby, can you please do the girls' hair?" From that day on, I never did my hair rebellion again. I kept loving and praying despite what "My momma said."

CHAPTER 5

Because the Family Structure Looks Different, the Principle Should Look How God Intended

Billy:

The order of the God-head relationship is God, then spouse, then children, then church, then everything else.

It usually takes about five years for a blended family to work as a traditional family, depending on how mature the individuals are. Through this book, we are believing to get some of those years back.

> **Exodus 34:14**
> *14 "For thou shalt worship no other god: for the LORD, whose name is Jealous, is a jealous God."*

I've seen so many cases where people put their children before their spouse, and it creates something called "legitimate jealousy," which is anything that took the spouse's place. That is out of order. In Scripture, the Word tells us God is a jealous

God, and no one should take His place. As Christ is the head of the church, so should the husband be the head of the house. So, ultimately, everyone tries to figure out where they fit in.

> **Genesis 2:24**
> **24** *"Therefore shall a man leave his father and his mother and shall cleave unto his wife: and they shall be one flesh."*

In our marriage, my wife and I planted in the children's minds, in their hearts that the husband and wife come before the children, church, the job, and everything else. We are one. However, the enemy's job is trying to keep us as two. In most peoples' marriages, spiritually, they are one—but physically, they are two.

There were moments in our marriage that, even though we said we came first, the enemy was always attacking us. He'd always start with the weakest link, and, at that time, it was me. I knew my wife said I came first, but it didn't seem like it as I'd make a decision that would be overridden. I would be asked questions like, "What do you think I should do?" then she would do the opposite. At the time, I wasn't respected as the head, and I felt like, "Why did you even ask me?"

In the beginning, the enemy and I stayed busy. I really didn't want to be what we called *home*. I had an ownership problem. My wife would say, take this to "my room" or "my this" or "my that." It bothered me so much that I didn't want to be in *her* house or deal with *her* kids.

In time, the house, the marriage, and the relationship were in a state of corrosion. I didn't want to be there. I had placed the job, my coaching, and everything else before my wife and kids. Then, infidelity stepped in on my part. Not knowing what to do, well, at this point, I was ready to throw in the towel. One of my sayings is, "I'm going to ride this train until the wheels fall off." Well, the wheels were falling off.

I was never home, even when my kids came over. I created ways to leave the house, and, most of the time, Shakerra would be home watching them. That was until something happened. I was called and told that Shakerra and the baby girl, Kyara, had gotten into it. Shakerra smacked Kyara, and then all hell had broken loose. This was a significant disaster in so many ways.

I realized it was all caused by the *head* being away from the home. My immaturity struck me, and I knew I must grow up quick, fast, and in a hurry. I was more concerned that now I had to deal with these kids' mom. Honestly, at that point, I didn't want to deal with her at all.

When I got to the house, I could feel the tension in the air, and I was trying to figure out how I could fix it. But, in the front of my mind was, "This is a way for me to escape." The way our rules were set up, when we were not at home, the oldest, Shakerra, was in charge; she made the decisions, but it never was to hit my kids. Kyara, being a handful, said whatever she wanted to—at her house. However, when she got smart with Shakerra, she smacked her. I asked Kerra why she hadn't called me. I could tell that Shakerra wasn't sure what I would do, but, ultimately, she loved her siblings, and she was going to discipline them. After all, she's the oldest.

Now before all this happened, it was already a tension-filled house. My marriage was on its last bolt, and the wheel was falling off. Shakerra got smart-mouthed mainly because she was hurt, needing a father figure. She felt her mother was being disrespected, and then *this joker* now comes before me!

I felt like all these kids came before me in action, so I told Shakerra, "If you don't like it, you can leave!" I already knew she really didn't have anywhere to go, but I was going to make her mother choose. I was so sure she was going to pick her daughter over me. The crazy thing was I wanted to leave, but I didn't have anywhere to go either. Shakerra said, "I'm not going anywhere." I said, "Great. Because I am!" I made a phone call, while packing my bags, to get someone to pick me up.

The house was in total turmoil; my wife didn't want me to leave, and the kids were crying as if we'd gotten a death call. It looked as if it was over, and the wheel had finally fallen off. But God interceded. My wife and I talked, and she found a place for Shakerra. I came back to the house because my wife understood the biblical principles and that the husband should come before the child.

We'd made a covenant that she was fulfilling… even if I wasn't. It had nothing to do with me. It was based on her relationship with God.

Tanisha:

Marriage alone is challenging, especially in the first five years. Marriage takes two mature individuals who understand the principles of working a marriage. Blending a family of four girls and one boy added to the new union. Nobody but Jesus saw us through. Parenting children in a traditional family is challenging, and some of the same violations that occur in a blended family happen just like in a conventional family. I said that to say, don't let no one tell you it can't work, it just takes work.

Billy:

We've worked through our ups and downs, and now we have the best marriage and relationship in this whole world. It's important not to make the children feel like you are choosing between them or your spouse, and this comes about through the maturity of the husband and wife. It's our priority to show our children the example of marriage as God intends it to be. Even though I know I am first but second to God, I understand the God-head, and truthfully, where I am at today, I wouldn't want to be with my wife if she put me before God. If she did, our relationship wouldn't last, anyway.

In many relationships, people have a hard time dealing with the order of priorities or how to transition. It goes like this: if you are not married and are in a relationship, your boyfriend or girlfriend does *not* come before your children. Both parties must understand that, including the children.

The problem is many people, such as my wife and I, have created soul ties before covenant ties. This put a strain on our marriage and caused significant confusion and conflict. Most in this situation never stay together long enough to get married.

Tanisha:

The day our lives changed forever—I remember it oh, so very well. Billy and I had a good day out. We had been shopping for new laptops and things for our business.

At home, there was tension in the air with Billy and the kids. Billy was very detached from the kids; more precisely, he was detached from the family altogether. I would check with him periodically and ask him if everything was okay, or did he need me to do more or less of something. His response always was, "No, everything is good; keep doing what you're doing." I would hear what he'd say, but his actions spoke differently. I stayed in prayer and continued seeking God's face.

On the day our lives changed, we were heading home when Billy's phone rung. Guess who it was? It was baby girl, and she was crying. She said Shakerra had smacked her. Immediately, the Holy Spirit let me know to brace myself. "It's about to go down," I heard. I had no idea what the Holy Spirit meant, but I braced myself. Billy was *angry.* I can't even say I wasn't mad because I wanted to beat her butt so many times. She needed it! But I never put my hands on her. I believe in beating that butt. The Bible tells you, in **Proverbs 13:24**, *"He that spareth his rod hateth his son: but he that loveth him chasteneth him betimes."* Then it says, in **Proverbs 23:13-14**, *"Withhold not correction from the child: for if you beatest him with the rod, he shall not die. Thou shalt beat him with the rod, and shalt deliver his soul from hell."*

So, it's against my religion not to beat that butt, because I love my kids and I don't want any of them to go to hell. Nevertheless, I had a sense of gratification. Sorry.

I raised my kids to be respectful to adults, even if the adult was wrong. Never have they ever got smart or done anything to disrespect Billy. But on this day, my eighteen-year-old daughter just *gave it* to Billy. I just stood there, bracing myself and watching. I did not interrupt. Shakerra and Billy were going back and forth, arguing. The other kids looked to be in a state of shock at what was taking place.

Shakerra said, "I don't like you, anyway." Mind you; she had seen Billy leave the house in the midnight hours or coming in the house at two or three a.m. She was eighteen; she knew that was wrong. She had lost all respect for him.

Billy's response to her was, "Well, you can get out." The kids started crying and everything. Shakerra said, " I'm not going nowhere. I'm staying here with my mom." Billy then said, "Cool. Well, I'm leaving."

Baby girl was crying, and she said, "No, Daddy, I didn't mean for this to happen." The house was in an uproar. Byron was on the stairs crying. He said, "Why can't we all just get along?" Meanwhile, I just stood there, watching, without a tear in my eyes. I told the kids to stop crying and that everything was going to be okay.

In front of Billy, I said, "No, Kerra. You're going to have to go. Billy's not leaving."

Through life, growing up, I'd seen many marriages destroyed by women putting their kids before their husbands. Most times, the families weren't even blended family homes, but some were. The kids would manipulate the whole situation to get their way, and most women fell for it every time. I always said I would not let any kids ruin my marriage. My kids would not come before my husband. I said that!

So, you know I got tried. My Lord, I got tried!

I stood for our marriage and, don't you know, Billy *still* left that night. My girlfriend, Kathy, took my kids for the weekend, and she let Shakerra move in with her. Tyana and Kyara went back home to their mother. I was home, all by myself.

Confused, numb, and in a fog, I texted Billy and said, "I stood for us, and you still left. Why???" That night, I got in the shower, and I just wept. I asked the Holy Spirit, "What just happened?" My heart.... I couldn't believe I'd put my oldest child out of the house. I cried as if someone had died. The Holy Spirit comforted me and reassured me that everything would be okay. I went from crying to praising God. I did not understand what was going on, but I had confidence in knowing that "all things work together for my good" (Rom. 8:28).

CHAPTER 6

The Challenges With Blended Families

Tanisha:

*W*e faced some challenges with our blended family when it came to the other parents. Unfortunately, my ex-husband could not deal with my husband, Billy, raising his son. When Billy and I got together, my son was three months old. Billy was there with him, full time. At the time, my ex was dealing with his struggles. Because of this, he was in and out of the kid's life. Once my son started talking, he started calling Billy, *Dad*. Mind you, no one in my house called him dad. My two girls were older, and they called him *Mr. Billy*. Tyana and Kyara mainly came over on the weekends in the early part of our relationship. My son could have picked it up from them. The bottom line was my ex, couldn't stand it.

My ex expressed to me that when he came to get Byron, he did not want to get him from Billy. It was just crazy because we were separated for fifteen months. He had several women in that time frame, and I never bothered him. Soon as I got with

Billy, the bull crap started. My mind was like, "We are getting a divorce, so what's the problem?"

There was never an issue where my two girls were concerned, and I guess it was because they were older. My ex just really had a problem with his son calling Billy Dad. He hated it so much that, one Sunday morning, he came to our house and asked to speak to Billy. My girls sat on the stairs and listened because their dad never talked to Billy, so they didn't know what was going on. He drove all the way to our house to ask Billy if he could stop Byron from calling him Dad. Billy said, "No. I will not because I didn't tell him to call me *Dad*. I'm not going to make him feel like I'm rejecting him." My kid's dad responded by asking, "How would you feel if your kids were calling another man *Dad*?" Billy said, "They do, but I'm secure in my spot." Then Billy said, "Shakerra calls you Dad." He responded, "Well, her dad wasn't there." Billy said, "And you weren't either."

The same was with Billy and the girl's mom. I figured we would have no problems because they had not been together for more than two years. Billy was in a relationship with someone else for those two years. So, "Why the drama, Jesus?"

Let me tell you the worst thing done, happened when we were about to get married. We were so excited. We knew just what we wanted and how we wanted it. We got our clothes tailor-made to our liking by this sweet lady we'd met, she truly was a blessing to us. Shakerra's dress was also custom-made by Mrs. Kathy. We had taken the other three girls to the store to find their dresses, and, oh, how beautiful they were. We had informed their mother we were going out looking for their dresses for the wedding. Then, on a separate day, we went to pick the girls up so we could find them shoes to wear with their dresses. The girls were excited about the wedding and being all dressed up and looking cute. I had decided that all four of our girls would get their hair done for the wedding as well. The week of our wedding, I talked with the girls' mom to decide for us to get them for wedding rehearsal on Thursday, and for me to pick them up halfway through the day from school on Friday, for the wedding. She agreed with everything.

Thursday evening, we called and called and called so we could get the girls for rehearsal—no answer. I figured maybe something happened. The coordinator was like, *"We can tell them what to do tomorrow."* "No problem! On the morning of the wedding, I called early to verify everything for that day. Well, guess what? No answer still. I called from approximately 7:30 am to 1:00 pm. No answer! The last call was around 1:00 pm, and I decided to leave a message.

I told my cousin, "Watch. She'll call back." Soon as I hung up from the message, a few seconds later, she called. I said to her, "I don't know why you are doing this; we have not done anything to you. But know this, you will reap what you sow."

She started saying something along the lines of, "If you would tell your husband—" I stopped her right there and said, "Are you going to let the girls be in the wedding?" She said, "No." I said, "Bye." I had to break the news to my husband. He was hurt.

I wasn't letting anyone or anything ruin my wedding day, so I didn't ponder on it at the time; I had things to do. My husband's best friend called and tried to talk to her, to convince her otherwise, but she wasn't hearing it. Billy asked if he could just at least talk to them, but she said, "No, they are at the babysitter's house." He asked for the babysitter's number so he could call them, but, once again, she refused.

My husband shed many tears on our wedding day because his daughters weren't allowed to be there with us. Nevertheless, they did get to wear their gowns and shoes at my Russell Family Reunion in Dallas, Texas, before they outgrew them.

CHAPTER 7

One-on-One Time With Your Bio-Child

Billy:

*P*hilippians 3:10 "And this, so that I may know Him [experientially, becoming more thoroughly acquainted with Him, understanding the remarkable wonders of His Person more completely] and [in that same way experience] the power of His resurrection [which overflows and is active in believers], and [that I may share] the fellowship of His sufferings, by being continually conformed [inwardly into His likeness even] to His death [dying as He did]."

In the passage above, the apostle Paul thought it was important to have one-on-one time with God. To know the Lord, you spend time with Him.

I remember, as a little boy, how I felt when my dad would pick me up for a visit, and it was just the two of us. I remember how he would give me his undivided attention—I didn't have to share him with anyone else. During those times, my dad would put me on his lap while driving, and I would steer the car around town while he pushed the gas pedal and brakes. I was too short for the pedals. He would "download" in my mind the directional skills then ask me, "Which way do I go—left or right?"

Anything I wanted to eat, he would get that for me, and he'd ask me all kinds of questions while we sat together. It was in those special times that our relationship was being built.

Forty-one years later, I still have those vivid memories. Dad would take me around to visit all his friends and brag on me, telling all his friends, "This is JR!" (Billy Dee Williams, Jr.) These days, my dad lives over 1,100 miles away. When I go visit him, he wants to take me around to see all his *shade-tree (a tree you sit under in the south)* friends. I didn't realize the importance of that because, later in life, I didn't see my dad very often. The most prolonged period of not seeing him was ten years, but I remember our one-on-one time, and that made all the difference. I knew he loved me, but it was difficult when he was around his wife and his blended family. I knew the difference, but couldn't articulate the feeling. I'm sure my dad was torn because he didn't know how to manage his blended family, and there was no one to show him.

One of my major regrets that I didn't figure out until later was that it was okay to spend one-on-one time with my kids. Even though I'd enjoyed that special time with my dad, it didn't occur to me to utilize that parenting tool with my own kids. As I look back on my life, my children were trying to tell me, and I was trying to say it, too. The problem was that none of us knew how to do it without offending the other spouse or the other kids.

There were times when I'd be driving my kids home, and it was just them and me. We had some of the greatest conversations then, which were all of ten minutes, and if we didn't catch the green traffic lights, twelve minutes. I remember feeling how I wished I could spend time with them alone. In fact, on their birthdays, somehow, I'd get away and spent one-on-one time with them, going to whatever restaurant they chose. We had a blast, but it felt like I was cheating, and many times, I had to downplay the moment because I didn't want it to seem like I'd had too much fun. It's one of the most awkward feelings in this world to have cheated on your wife and other kids by spending time alone with one kid. If you've ever felt like that, it is out of order.

To have a successful, blended family—especially when the children are younger—relies on the adults understanding this reasoning. Each parent should allow the other spouse to do this, to spend personal time with their children, without anyone getting jealous or ruining plans.

If you really want to be mature about it and make our enemy (satan) mad, then encourage this free time. If need be, help finance it. Before you do this, make sure you two, as a couple, are secure in each other. It is each adult's responsibility to make sure that nobody can or will take each other's place, especially from the baby momma or baby daddy. (That's a whole other book.)

Last year, in 2018, Kyara, the baby girl, having turned eighteen, drove with me to Arkansas to drop my dad off after a visit. He'd stayed three weeks with me for the first time in my life, and me being forty-one years old, I still longed to spend one-on-one time with my father.

The trip back was one of the greatest accomplishments of my life. For once, I didn't feel like I was cheating, and Kyara and I had an amazing time together. It was just the two of us, driving 1,100 miles together in one car. I got to see her face and her expressions. Little things, like what she snacks on, came into focus, but more importantly, the feeling of driving on the big highways brought back memories of when I was a little boy. Those special times that my dad had me sit on his lap and allow me to steer the car while giving me driving *nuggets*, those are the special times that I remember to this day. I was able to instill that in Kyara, telling her she drives like a champ—I guess she gets it from her daddy, lol.

Kyara was affected the most by not spending one-on-one time with her. Growing up, she had built up anger against me, and, to be truthful, she really didn't want anything to do with me. She is my only biological child, but I have spent so much time, energy with other people and other kids that she didn't know the man those other people spoke of. She grew bitter towards me.

I remember trying to get that relationship up and running, so I text her that I wanted our relationship to grow and to get better. Her response was, "Why now?"

The only thing I could think of was 1) I'm still living, 2) you're still living, 3) I love you more you can imagine, and 4) God is still in control.

I had to go through the rejection and understand how she was feeling; hurt people hurt people, but I never gave up. I look back on when I went out of town, Tanisha would lay in the bed with her kids. They'd watch movies and have a ball together. They would go to many places with her without a thought of "no." They loved each other and spend time together when I was gone. They got to have their mother all to themselves. But to accomplish it, it felt strange. We didn't know we shouldn't be feeling this way, and no one was there to tell us it was okay.

It was creating an unhealthy family. We began to buy them stuff secretly but feel guilty afterward.

Tanisha:

I really wish we knew more about how to do this part, as it was a tough thing for me to figure out. With no one to teach us about this, we had to wing it. I cried many times, just trying to find a balance between my husband, my kids, my mom, and myself. It was nerve-wracking sometimes, trying to be everything for everyone and not let anyone feel slighted.

I loved the times when it was my kids laying up in the bed watching movies with me. We only got to do that when Billy was away. When he was away, all three of my kids slept in bed with me. We might go somewhere in the car, just us four— talking, laughing and just catching up with each other. We did that as a family, also, when all seven of us were together. We could have had more one-on-one time if we had known it was okay and healthy to have that alone time with just one child.

There were times when my husband wanted to get away for a few days. I always tried to take the kids because I felt so guilty leaving them home. We made many mistakes learning how to blend our family, but LOVE carried the weight, and we made it through. To God, be the glory!

Chapter 8

Let the Bio Do the Discipline

Billy:

This is, by far, is one of the most difficult things to do in a blended family, and age has a lot to do with it. Love must be established *before discipline;* the new blended family and the child will let you know when it is time. But until then, let the "Bio Parent" do the disciplining, mainly because the children know that their mom or dad loves them without question. Also, they have already built a rapport with this parent.

What makes this so difficult is that many are trying to discipline but haven't established love where the kids know, and the new parent knows it. I might make a note of this: every child is different. There is one vital role you play, and both parties must be in agreement, especially when it comes to discipline. Tanisha was the disciplinarian for two reasons: 1) she loves it, and 2) her absolute favorite scripture is Proverbs KJV 13:24, *"He that spareth his rod hateth his son: but he that loveth him chasteneth him betimes."* If there is no other scripture she knows, she knows this one.

I have been laid back as far as discipline in the area of corporal punishment. I was the *fun parent* and tried to find another means to discipline the kids. Well, mainly, it was a childhood issue, because I got beat so much as a child, I promised the Almighty God that I wouldn't hit my children like I'd been beaten. Even to this day, if someone raises their hand real fast, I flinch. So, that carried over to my relationship with Tanisha.

There was a period I didn't have my kids and another when I started getting them consistently. I had to build a relationship with them before I began beating their backsides. During those times, Tanisha was so upset at me. She thought the kids were off the hook, and they need a beating right now—and she was right—but what she didn't understand was she had never left her kids. She'd always been in her kids' lives, always built a rapport with her kids, and they knew their mom's favorite scripture, too.

The reason for my madness was that I only got my children on weekends, and I still was building a foundation of love. I didn't care what anyone thought or how they felt, because they were my children. I thought, "What if Tanisha and I don't work out? I'm going to lose you and my kids, and now I'm all by myself." So, after a while, when I thought I'd given the right amount of warnings, I started beating those backsides and, boy, did things change. It was one of the worst times of my life because I had to pray to God to help me beat my kids' backside. When they'd leave the room, I would be emotionally weak.

Tanisha:

This area was a big problem for me. For example, I didn't play the hitting game. First, they are playing, and when someone is crying. So after a few times of me disciplining my girls after an incident, Billy would just talk to his two girls, we had a problem. His explanation of why he wasn't beating their butt didn't work for me because those children needed a beating. I told my girls if they hit you again, hit them back. I was not getting in it.

One day, after I gave the green light, I guess Byrianna hit somebody hard because I got a phone call from the girls' mother. She told me she didn't agree with kids disciplining kids. I said, "Well, evidently, you don't agree with adults doing it either because Billy doesn't discipline them and neither do you so I told my daughters, "if the girls are big enough to pass a lick, they are big enough to get hit back."

I raised my kids never to start trouble and that if someone hit them, for them to tell someone. But if they tell someone and nothing is being done, then Nah, we're not having this. Problems!!! Furthermore, my girls would see Billy disciplining Byron, but not his girls. Oh my God, they were mad about that. What we explained to them was that Billy had raised Byron from the time he was three months old, and he's with him full time. Byron loves Billy, and Byron knows Billy loves him. The problem is we didn't communicate that to the girls until later.

My advice on the topic, please communicate beforehand disciplining the children and be on the same page. You must communicate this to the children as well.

Chapter 9

Never Compete With the Other Parent.

Billy

It is too funny and immature when you see or hear others competing with their counterparts. You must know *who you are as a person*, or you will find yourself in a contest of *who is the better parent*. Whoever wins is the Biggest Loser. What you will find out later is that material things are not love, and all kids want is love. The biggest loser is the parent who tries to outdo the other parent by giving material stuff.

Another pitfall: it's too often the situation where the one parent tries to compare themselves with the other parent by putting the other parent down. A friend of mine got caught up in a competing war within a blended family. The child would say something like, *he or she bought me this*. Then, the child would get something bigger and better from the other parent trying to outdo him. Well, in the beginning, that child is winning because they're getting everything they ask for and more until something happens where one of the parents can't afford it.

In this case, time is not money. Many kids grow up and say, "I'd rather had time together than money." I see people pay child support, but never spend their time or attend any of their child's functions. Quality time outweighs the quality of a dollar.

I see and hear parents talk about the other parent in front of the children—this is entirely out of order. There are things I didn't like that my kids' mom did or said. I've never tried to defend myself because, as long as God knew, the truth would come out eventually. I don't like hearing parents use their kids as a pawn or want to be the so-called "better parent." I often hear parents getting into arguments because the child's hair is done a certain way or for not using the right shampoo or conditioner or oil sheen.

When Byron was much younger, I had so much sympathy for his father as a man and could understand what he was feeling. For many years, I have been my own barber and cut hair for many others. It's a trade I picked up when I was younger. When my mom couldn't afford to send me to the barber and didn't know anyone who could cut my hair, she'd cut it with scissors. It was one of the worst parts of my life—I looked horrible—so I learned how to cut my hair. My son, while growing up, his hair was *wolfing* (looking really rough). He looked like a cute monster, but I didn't want to take that away from his father because of sentimental value. I was so secure in my spot, but his father wasn't. Sounds crazy, but I did think about how that would make him feel if I'd cut his son's hair for the first time. What's sad is, it took me a while to blend in, but I didn't want his father to think I was competing with him. It just so happens that I love his kids, too, and it's not my fault that they're not together.

Never Compete With the Other Parent.

I went as far as not even potty training my son Byron because I wanted his father to do that and build a relationship as father and son. I always thought that my son could have the best of both worlds. What I didn't know was what his birth father could teach him and what his birth father didn't know I could teach our son.

My two girls had another father (Tyana, Kyara), and as long as he respected my girls, I was cool; I stayed out of the way. I've always told my girls to respect their mom's husband because I know how it feels to be the other guy. To be perfectly honest, I never had a problem with them calling him *Dad* because I knew who I was, and the DNA tests said I was 9999999.9999999% the father. Although, I didn't need that to know that she was my child. I still felt my girls could have a unique situation—let's come together for the sake of the children and make the best of it.

What's upsetting is, if you try to compete and can't, you end up fading away. It's ultimately about the children, and too many people make it a competition. Then we lose the kids. If you put the time in with your children, especially when they are younger, you impact their life so much it doesn't matter what anyone else says; they know the truth.

One of my biggest regrets was that I didn't fight for my girls when they were younger. I had gotten a court order to get them from Wednesday to Sunday every week. But, I didn't want the cops involved or my kids to see that kind of forced interaction. I kind of gave them a choice. Tyana was much closer to me, she always wanted to come, but Kyara never really wanted to, but she did. When things didn't go the way she wanted, she secretly called or texted her mom, and the next thing you know, they were leaving. At the time, it looked as if it backfired on me, but the true and living God worked it out. Tyana, in her senior year of high school, moved with us, and I took her to school every day, including school, on Saturday until she graduated. She is currently in the U.S. Navy. Kyara decided after her first year of college to move in with us as well.

CHAPTER 10

Family Meeting Bridge the Gaps

Billy

*A*long this journey, what has sustained us, with the help of God, is family meetings.

My wife and I had never heard of family meetings unless there was a death in the family. Even then, I was never included. As a child, no matter the decisions made, I would find out in the process and do as I was told because I was a child.

A lot of times, we talk to couples that are having significant issues, and one of the questions we ask is, "Do you have family meetings?" What people miss is that it helps the child to gain understanding at their level. It teaches them the importance of gathering to discuss what has happened and what is about to happen.

No matter what, the parent is supposed to have the final say. It's essential to have a family meeting so you can find out what the child is thinking. Not only that, but it makes the child feel that what they have to say is important.

Through family meetings, I found out my children expected me to be at their functions but also wanted their father there. I found out how my new, blended family felt when I would come home, head straight to my room, and never spend time with them unless my kids came over. They were able to see the difference. It's how I found out how my kids felt about their new siblings. It's how I found out Baby Girl thought my wife was mean; she felt as if she was always being picked on and not loved.

Now, remember, this was all new to us. We had never heard of a traditional family having family meetings and especially not blended families. We knew it was important to sit them down and hear them out, but they also could hear us out. If anyone intended to stay at our house for a lengthy time, we would talk to the kids first before we gave a final decision. Except there was one time, I just did it and made a final decision on my own. The whole house was uncomfortable. I used my *head of the house* authority, and that was entirely out of order.

Any major decisions that need to be made, my wife and I talk about first, then we discuss it with the kids and see what they think. During my last hospital visit, the doctor called me and said I needed to go to the emergency room ASAP based on my previous blood work. I discussed it with my wife, then I had a family meeting and told them the process. The kids just want to be a part of things, and I believe it's so important to communicate the next move.

It's not the responsibility of one parent or the other to initiate the meeting as long as it gets done. We can spend so much valuable time trying figure who is going to do it—just be in agreement. Sometimes, my wife will initiate it, but most of the time, I will conduct and end it. Most of the time, I open in prayer, and my wife closes in prayer.

Remember, you're setting a standard not only for your kids but for the next generation. My kids can never say they never had a family meeting. All meetings haven't been peaches and cream, but we've gotten to discuss some exciting things, too, like family vacations — more on that in the next chapter.

Chapter 11

The Importance of Family Vacations

Billy:

Family vacations were the glue that held our family together. We didn't have much, but we had each other, and we were going to make the best out of it. We didn't let what we *didn't have to* get in the way of what we did—which was love. We would take two and three vacations in a hotel with two beds, and it would be just us. Some kids would sleep on the floor, and some would be on the bed. One time we got a hotel room with a television in the bathroom mirror. My son took his blanket and watched TV there. We would buy a bunch of snacks and hang out. Some of our best vacations were when we would wing it.

Man, my kids stayed ready. They would load the board games up in a heartbeat. I believe that was the fastest time we ever got everyone in the car and didn't forget anything and didn't have to wait for anybody.

As I discussed in the previous chapter concerning vacations, the meetings were where we planned our extended stays—where we were going and when we were going. We never had any drama with the other parent concerning that; it was great.

There was a certain ritual we did on long road trips. We fried a bunch of chicken and made a bunch of sandwiches before we left. Then we bought plenty of junk food because we couldn't afford to go out to eat in restaurants while on the road.

I did most of the driving. I would pray before we left, and I preferred to leave at night, so I could drive the most miles while they slept. We have always allowed our kids to be themselves, and, unfortunately, they are very loud even to this day—most of them thought they were grown. We would sing on the road, play different games on the road, and they would get on my everlasting nerves asking, "Dad, how long we got?" That is until they got cellphones, then they can look their own travel time up.

We knew the importance of this so we would take once-a-year vacations with the kids and several as a couple, but also many two-and three-day getaways, which we discussed earlier. I believe a family that plays together stays together! You can't be so serious about everything and miss the process of having fun.

When I look back at what all we have done, it was nobody but God. Our last family vacation with everyone was one that we planned. We knew this could be the last one with just us seven— five kids and two parents. In this planning process, they wanted nobody but us; my mother-in-law would go on most of our trips, but "not this time" said the kids. They just wanted us. It was the wisest decision they've ever made.

The Importance of Family Vacations

We decided to go to the Poconos in Pennsylvania, which was a destination for a couple of our trips. The kids were much older at this point, and we had made it through the most challenging part of our life as a family. Shakerra was back home from missionary school for good, and Tyana had just signed up for the US Navy. We'd just finished our first year as the First Family of Love Oasis Ministries. We needed some time away. As of this writing, it was, by far, the best trip ever. We did everything together—we laughed and reminisced about the things we've shared in this book, and it has made us who we are today.

That vacation gave us a sense of relief, we'd made it through all the drama and could laugh and talk about it. You know you're healed when old stories no longer affect you the way they did before.

CHAPTER 12

You Can Be Blended and Not Broken

Billy:

In this chapter, I'd like to encourage someone that may be broken and blended. By now, you should know that God is a Restorer and a Redeemer, but it comes at the expense of both parents giving up immaturity. My wife and I believe in the Promise, but the process almost did us in. It's going to take a lot of love, forgiveness, and patience. At some point, we, as parents, must be able to hear the children and see their behavior. The truth of the matter is, it's the adults who decided to have children. The kids only go along the ride and have no clue about the final destination because we, as parents, think it's none of their business, but the children are affected the most.

I highly recommend that if you are dating, don't be so quick to introduce that special person to your kids, mainly because, what if this woman or man doesn't work out? Then, your kids have become emotionally involved, thinking he or she is about to make their mother or father happy, and it doesn't turn out to be the case. What a lot of people don't understand is that it could take up to five years for a blended family to look or perform as a traditional family.

Tanisha:

In the times we live in now, people quit and give up at the drop of a dime. Giving up is easy; it's staying in and fighting that takes work. First off, I don't believe many understand the covenant of marriage and the vows that they took before God and the people. You said for better or for worse, for richer or for poorer, in sickness and in health, forsaking all others......my God. You will have challenges, you will bend, you will want to throw in the towel, but I'm here to tell you, blended or not, you will face the same obstacles.

Don't break, work on you, build your relationship with God, walk in the principles of God's Word, and watch it work! It does no good just to know God's Word; you must work the word! Allow the Holy Spirit to lead and guide you; He will not let you down. If I had not had a relationship with the Holy Spirit, hearing and following His voice, I would not be married today! But that's another book.

CHAPTER 13

From the Children's Perspective

Byrianna:

I am the second oldest in our blended family. I believe I was eight, turning nine when our parents married. I love my family, but blending this thing was not as easy as we have made it look over the years.

I remember being told from peers that they wished they had my family. I would look at them as if they were crazy. I'd then tell them *you do not know the struggle, God graced us to make it work as we do*.

Growing up in a blended family had its ups and downs. It didn't help that our clan was made up of mostly females, four girls, and one boy, who was also the baby. Having a gang of girls would drive a nuclear family crazy, so you can only imagine how my childhood went.

Speaking of crazy, I guess I will start with the downs of growing up *blended*. Having to merge four different personalities was probably one of the biggest cons of being in my blended family.

Especially since my mother was a strong disciplinarian, and my two bonus sisters were raised in a completely different household than us. Things my siblings and I would get chastised about or even beatings for; they would only get talked to, and I didn't understand that. They needed their behinds whooped! My bonus sisters had smart mouths, and we were taught not to challenge anyone older than you. It didn't matter if it was an adult or not if they were older than you, you respected them, point-blank. Period.

But those little girls gave us a run for our money. It is safe to say we had a lot of arguments and misunderstandings. Some were minutes, and others made lasting impressions on the structure of our family. Although we fought and argued, the good outweighed the bad. The pros of gaining two extra siblings were worth the petty battles we went through.

Yes, we fought, but we played and joked even harder. We always came up with something to do. I also loved the family trips we'd take every year. Some of our best memories were during family trips.

I also enjoyed having two extra people to have my back and vice versa. We didn't always get along or like each other, but we never let anyone mess with one of us. You had a problem with one you were going to catch *a case* with the rest of us. We were, and still are, like a gang. That is one of my favorite parts of being blended. I love all my siblings, and blood couldn't make the bond we share any closer. Everything we went through only made us closer, and we have the legendary family meetings to thank for that.

My advice to couples that are planning on blending a family would be to set up playdates for the kids before you even say, "I do." Let your children get to know each other just like you guys date and court to get to know each other. If the kids build a friendship first, it will be easier to adjust as a family because they already like each other. Becoming a family would be the icing on the cake.

Now, the advice I'd give to the kids would be to be patient and understanding. Your parents only want what's best for you and might not get it right the first time.

Tyana:

Growing up in a blended family was difficult, in my experience. I was able to conform and be cordial; however, I was the older sister on my mom's side. That made it almost heartbreaking when my younger sister constantly felt unaccepted by the blended side. It made it extremely hard to build a bond with my bonus siblings while also trying to stick up for my own sister and give her constant reassurance that it's completely okay to be and stay true to herself.

After all, our bonus siblings weren't changing their ways, especially for children who were being thrown into a completely new way of life for a weekend. So, my sister shouldn't have had to either. I sort of felt like the *bridge sibling*. I felt like I was mature enough to hear out both sides, understand them, and know why they thought the way they did. My goal was to combine them through playing.

Pros and cons. Pros included in an extended family are, you have more people to love and support you. Pros can also include seeing and being raised in a healthy household. Cons could be a conflict between the way a child is accustomed to being raised versus new rules they're forced to adapt to. Cons can even be clashing and conflicting personalities in the home.

To the parents blending a family, I advise you to try to understand your bonus child's (or children's) current way of life. See what they may like and try to accentuate that to form a bond. Also, try to find an understanding of their upbringing and ease your own alterations on them, if need be. Don't just force things on them and expect them to take it in with open arms. Never make a child feel unwanted or unloved or left out. It will leave a bad taste in their mouth that's hard to get rid of. Children need to feel love. If nothing else in the world, a child needs love to grow and flourish.

To children merging into a blended family, my advice to you is to be the best you, still. Find where you stand out and exceed there. If your new parent makes you feel some type of way, communicate that whether it's the way they speak to you, how they make you feel, or if you feel excluded from your own family. Keep the best open lines of communication, even when you don't want to. It will make your transition go a lot smoother, and it will impact the bond you will develop with your new family.

Kyara:

Growing up in a blended family was extremely hard for me. Out of all five children, I believe I felt it the most and for the longest. I felt like there was another woman who wanted to take the place of my mother. My mother was my world, so I felt offended in a sense, and I resented my "stepmother."

Also, at home, my sister and I had a lot of freedom. YES, we had boundaries, but, YES, my mother allowed us to be kids. I never noticed the freedom until I would go to my dad's house, and I realized we were not able to do anything. I loved to laugh and play, have a good time, and go places, but I felt like, on the weekends, when I was with my dad, I was unable to do anything that made me happy. I grew up hating the weekends! Just about everything I wanted, I was told not to do, it caused me to be closed and not ask for anything.

Growing up in a blended family had many pros and cons. Fortunately, in our situation, throughout all the years on this rollercoaster, the pros surpassed my cons. Throughout this whole process, I gained another mother, two sisters, a brother, and a host of family members I feel have genuinely loved and supported me. It also strengthened the bond between my biological sister and me because we could always vent to one another. No one understood what we were going through as we did.

I was disciplined in a way that built me up as a person and for my future. I was taught valuable lessons. I was shown the true essence of love, family, and coming together. But most importantly, I was able to develop my own personal relationship with God throughout it all.

The advice I would give to the parents would be, if you are coming out of a relationship with their other parent, explain to the child why it didn't work. Most people like to keep everything in the dark about divorces or breakups, and that is okay for the world—but not for your children. Of course, keep it age-appropriate, but this is very important for them to understand, so they do not grow up questioning what happened or themselves. Sit down and talk to your own children before they meet your boyfriend or girlfriend. Let them understand how you feel about the person you are dating and allow them room to react. Encourage them to explain how they feel and let them voice their opinion. Although you are in love, listen to your child, because the process will affect them and the relationship between you two for the rest of your life.

If I talked to children within blended families, I would tell them to be patient. This whole process is as new to them as it is their parents. Neither of their parents ever would've planned for this to be the outcome, but they are learning how to handle this situation the best they possibly know-how. I would also say, LOVE your parents enough to want what is best for them, what makes them happy, and respect who they love. Parents never go into a blended family to hurt or destroy their child or children. Your parents have fallen in love. They feel safe, comfortable, and are in love—this is all they are trying to pursue. I know, growing up in a blended family, I never looked at this side of it. My father was joined with a woman, and I was so selfish and ignorant in the sense that I could not see how they felt for each other, but only what I was feeling in the process as if it was easy for them.

www.ingramcontent.com/pod-product-compliance
Ingram Content Group UK Ltd.
Pitfield, Milton Keynes, MK11 3LW, UK
UKHW022216230426
12048UKWH00016BA/887